Washington

Homes on Prince Street in Alexandria were built by
sea captains in the 1700s, while the cobblestone streets
were reportedly laid by Hessian soldiers during the
American Revolution.

Washington

JOAN SCHREINER MANN

Photos by Milt and Joan Mann

KODANSHA INTERNATIONAL LTD.
TOKYO, NEW YORK & SAN FRANCISCO

Distributed in the United States by Kodansha International/USA Ltd. through Harper & Row, Publishers, Inc., 10 East 53rd Street, New York, New York 10022.

Published by Kodansha International Ltd., 12-21, Otowa 2-chome, Bunkyo-ku, Tokyo 112 and Kodansha International/USA Ltd., 10 East 53rd Street, New York, New York 10022 and 44 Montgomery Street, San Francisco, California 94104. Copyright in Japan 1973 by Kodansha International Ltd. All rights reserved. Printed in Japan.

LCC 73-79764
ISBN 0-87011-211-2
JBC 0326-784188-2361

First edition, 1973
Second printing, 1981

Contents

To
Sylvia and Arthur Broida
Margaret and Robert Paul
Marta and Louis Schreiner

Congress's Town

FOUR and one half centuries ago, Ponce de Leon was directed by friendly Caribbean natives to fabled lost cities of gold. If he were to come back today and ask for similar directions from the native American taxpayer, he would undoubtedly be directed to Washington, District of Columbia, for in the mind of that taxpayer, no other city is the source of so many gold-plated fairy tales as the Federal City. In a similar vein, the city has also been known in recent times as Camelot, supposedly a place where aristocrats live and rule in glory while the rest of the "kingdom" is forgotten. Washingtonians, however, draw parallels to Disneyland; it is, they say, a funland attracting those from the outside, who come looking for dreams without realizing that the price of participation is high.

Most of Washington is wedged between the Potomac and Anacostia rivers on what used to be tobacco fields, fruit orchards and swamp. To Algonquian-speaking Indians, the longer river was a *potomack,* or "trading place." Meandering from its origins in the Appalachian Mountains along the Piedmont Plateau, the Potomac reaches sea level near Arlington Memorial Bridge. Long the favorite of Georgetown University rowing teams, boating remains the only form of recreation, since bacterial contamination has made it hazardous to humans and fish.

Captain John Smith was the earliest recorded Anglo-Saxon sightseer. In 1608, he sailed up the Potomac as far as Great Falls, one of the many waterfalls that define the Fall Line, the geological boundary between the mountains, an hour's drive from the capital, and the Coastal Plain, of which the District of Columbia occupies sixty-nine square miles cut out of the State of Maryland.

"Hydrometeorologist's heaven" is the way one employee of the National Oceanic and Atmospheric Administration lovingly billed D. C. Then he continued with the inevitable statistics: "Average temperature 66° F; low 48° F. Weather is generally mild with no more than twenty inches of snow in a good winter. The rest of the time it's hot, humid and rainy." To some that might explain the irrationality of the governing body. Short tempers are kept hotter in the winter by an overdose of heat in government buildings and are somewhat cooled at other times by overwork and air conditioners.

Perhaps if the latter had been available in 1861, D. C. would not have become the emblem of the North while right across the Potomac, Virginia was a bastion of Confederate rebels. Arlington Memorial Bridge spiritually symbolizes the missing link in the ideological gap. "Notice," rambled a tour guide, "how it connects Lincoln Memorial to Arlington House, once the home of Robert E. Lee." Tourists may envision the nine graceful arches of concrete as the binder of wounds, and local residents know that the five-minute trip will envelop them in an aura from the days when the viability of the republic was in doubt.

When it comes to pride of place, Virginians rank with Texans as the proudest people in the Union, although they may wince at the last word. Replies to questions concerning their origins are invariably delivered in a patient, and, to our Midwestern ears, condescending Southern drawl, "From Virginia, Suh!"

The irregular circle of black, white and green that cinches within its confines Washington and its environs—the seventh largest and fastest growing metropolitan area in the country, 2.5 million people expected to swell to 4 million in 1980—is called the Capital Beltway. It acts as the main feeder for the subassembly lines crisscrossing the area and carrying workers into the machinery that runs the country.

Washington was unique at its inception in that no modern nation prior to 1800 had built a city for the sole purpose of being the seat of its government. Although the founding fathers envisioned industrial growth, Washington has remained a city whose prime industry is bureaucracy. Some light industry has recently invaded the suburbs. Since environmentalists term it clean, the only conclusion to be drawn is that traffic is the main reason why Washington, when not sitting in the mist of rain, is shrouded in pollution. Even the Lincoln Memorial is beginning to show the effects. National Park Service officials were reluctant to admit that one of the reasons for closing the traffic circle around the monument was that they suspected exhaust fumes were taking a toll on the building.

Surprisingly, mother nature is holding her own. Parks constituting much of the city are emerald in summer and by October are well covered with the reds and yellows and oranges of maple, elm and oak. However, what mother nature proposes, Congress disposes. And it is probably through one of its famous "acts of" that gardeners vacuum the streets and sidewalks around government buildings to remove fallen leaves.

The anomaly of the nation's capital is its own government: it is a "colony" of the federal government, a congressional company town that has to beg, borrow and rely on the nation's legislators for every morsel necessary to finance its operation. "It would take an act of Congress" is an expression for describing any task of gargantuan proportions, and here such an act lies behind everything, from erecting public buildings to kite-flying permits.

Home rule has been a thorn in the hearts of Washingtonians since they lost the right to elect city officials in 1871. When the city was incorporated on May 3, 1802, the president appointed the mayor, while the people were allowed to elect city councilmen. From 1812 to 1820, the council elected the mayor. The only period during which both council and mayor were popularly elected was from 1820 to 1871.

Excuses as to why that form of government was abandoned have been muddled, but eventually they boil down to the fact that congressional committees in charge of the city were headed by men with the most seniority, who were consistently Southerners. Besides having to live with the Emancipation Proclamation, they were alarmed at the increasing rate at which freed slaves poured in. In what they regarded as a patriotic move to keep the city red, blue and very white, they enacted a territorial form of government. The governor and his eleven-member council became presidential appointees.

During President Lyndon B. Johnson's term of office a new form of commissioner-council was initiated. The presidentially appointed office of commissioner fell to a large, affable man with an appropriate surname, Walter E. Washington. Although it is not his proper title, everyone refers to him as Mayor Washington. Militant blacks rejoiced at what they felt was a positive move, but the mayor's effectiveness in running the city is severely limited. Politically hamstrung, he spends most of his time artfully dodging criticism and fencing with congressmen in efforts to obtain the one-billion-dollar annual budget. He and his staff must prepare appeals to the District of Columbia committees of the House and Senate for favorable legislation; then to put approved plans into effect, they must justify requests for appropriations before other committees of Congress.

Adding to financial problems, the federal government sits on approximately 43 percent of prime city land and has ruled another 8 percent tax exempt. Yet the government pays only 14 percent of general revenues, thus requiring the appointed city government to propose additional appeals for each specific project.

The imminent return of the district to a home rule of sorts will do nothing to loosen Congress's hold on the purse strings, but the popularly elected mayor and city council will provide residents with a voice in local affairs.

Despite its inner conflicts, placid is the best word to describe Washington. At the southern end of the eastern megalopolis, it is the country cousin, lacking the historicity of Boston, the sophistication of New York and the industry of Baltimore. Its architectural contours are gratefully unaffected by the towering steel eruptions favored by contemporary metropolitan builders. Only Washington Monument and the Capitol rise above the limits set by law on building heights, which can be no more than the width of the street on which they stand. Translated grudgingly by architects and contractors, the limit averages 130 feet except along a section of Pennsylvania Avenue, where a 160-foot height is permitted. Although both groups bemoan the regulations by which they are bound, they like to work here. No matter how many experts praise or denounce their dreams, in the end it is Congress that bears the brunt of criticism, since the funds it appropriates are invariably insufficient.

Noon, when people pour from their offices into downtown restaurants and nearby parks, is the city's busiest hour. Few come into the city once the din of the evening rush hour has subsided. Washington keeps a poorly lit eye open to watch those daring enough to tread its streets after dark. By 1 A.M., traffic signals blink on nearly empty streets, as the infrequent late imbiber hastily crosses midtown in search of refuge.

It is difficult to believe that the eighth most crime-ridden city in the country had but one policeman in 1811. Today, after monuments, blue uniforms are its most prominent feature. The law enforcement list appears unending, starting with the metropolitan and National Park Service police, who are the most numerous. Each branch of the government (legislative, executive and judicial) has its own in addition to the Federal Protective Service, which keeps tabs on government property. Of course, there are the specialists, the Federal Bureau of Investigation and the Secret Service, but to insure a fail-safe system, some government agencies do not hesitate to hire private security services. Recent figures show that the efforts of the Metropolitan Police to curb lawlessness are having their effects. However, these problems are a rapidly increasing plague of the suburbs.

Civil rights movements and the Vietnam conflict brought a flood of protestors. To counteract rambunctious demonstrators, a well-trained riot squad was developed with the aid of those experts in disorder control, the Tokyo police.

Civil rights demands also opened the door to more black police recruits. Blacks now comprise 40 percent of the force, although complaints still ripple that advancement is slow. Questioned as to why more blacks do not join the force, one officer shrugged it off as being "a particularly unpopular vocation within the black community."

The National Park Service's mounted police are the most visible, their stamping grounds being the Mall and the Ellipse. Few mounted police applicants are drawn from the long waiting list, as there are only twenty-eight saddles and two sergeant positions available. An intensive sixty-day training course thoroughly prepares a man to care for himself and his animal. Horses, young, spotlessly black, usually quarter or at least part thorough-bred are trained by their eventual masters. "The important thing," said one policeman, "is that the horse never lose its cool in the mess of summer traffic." He was a firm believer in the benefits of a mounted corps.

"This height gives me a vantage point capable of surveying over the tops of cars for suspicious situations. Summer traffic is so thick that even a motorcycle officer has difficulty maneuvering. For me a quick gallop across the grass can solve a problem. Do you know," he said, stretching down to place a ticket on a Pinto, "that one well-trained mounted rider can replace thirty, fifty officers on foot? Few people argue with a horse, even those who understand them."

He went on to cite their public relations value. "Policemen in uniform have a bad reputation today. But one on a horse still sits pretty tall in anyone's saddle."

Casually he rode away, heading towards a group of boisterous kids free at last from the rigors of museum viewing. All stopped, stunned for a moment, then ran to the curb for a closer look. They tottered back and forth in their sneakers with delight, eyes popping, mouths ajar. All the treasures of the Smithsonian forgotten, a horse and rider became the experience of the day.

Washingtonians are amazingly friendly. Perhaps it is their proximity to politicians that makes them exceptionally verbal. They are also more aware of current news events than any other Americans.

Two major newspapers provide them with the details, the *Star-News* and the *Washington Post*; the latter is rated as one of America's finest dailies. Yet both lack the human touch of the *Shepherd Street News* of suburban Chevy Chase, Maryland. This weekly, a single sheet of legal-sized paper, is mimeographed by six very young aspiring newspapermen and a flock of highly underpaid junior reporters. Subscriptions at twenty cents per month cannot cover everything!

The Shepherd Street News concentrates on very local current events: "The Whites of Turner Lane are varnishing their door. ... The Fleischman's cat Gonzales got hit by a car three weeks ago. It is almost better now." It also dispenses sage advice to the young: "Some kids threw eggs at some of the stores on Brookville Road last Saturday. The windows are eggy [*sic*]. We think that was a bad thing to do!"

All three newspapers aid the Washingtonian in his favorite pastime, spreading rumors. No one escapes gossip, whether cornered in person or via the ubiquitous cord that links all souls together, the telephone. In providing this overused necessity, the telephone company has been more than generous. Talk is cheap. Flat rates cover one of the largest metropolitan networks in the country. A thin dime suffices, even across state lines into the surrounding Virginia and Maryland suburbs, unless the caller is trying to deal with a government agency. Then eight or ten dimes may be necessary: it usually takes that number of functionaries to solve any one problem.

Lonely souls without hearing impairments can easily find friends in a variety of recorded messages. Besides the usual prayers, weather and the ever-sympathetic Alcoholics Anonymous, there is a number to bring the word from the Democratic National Committee, and others deliver messages from various legislators. Those who want to know the latest in government happenings but prefer not to be bogged down in party rhetoric can dial 223–0580, which automatically denotes the status of various bills before Congress.

The basis for most local gossip is money, principally an individual's civil service rating. Nowhere else in the nation is one so conscious of what his neighbor earns. Government funding of its agencies is also a matter of individual concern. The large number of research scientists in government employ is a case in point. Employees of the National Aeronautics and Space Administration, for example, walk the thin line of financial insecurity as Congress frequently cuts back funds while deciding whether the next batch of moon rocks will be worth the expense. Similarly, the National Institutes of Health, where the continual assault on disease would hardly appear to benefit from budgetary squabbles, is plagued with unfinished research, as, under the prodding of special interest groups, funding for one malady is dropped in favor of another.

This unstable bookkeeping tends to put many Washingtonians on the transient list. It is estimated that 25 percent of the population never unpacks its bags, and D. C. ranks with the states of Hawaii and New York in having more renters than homeowners.

Georgetown is the landlord's dream. During the 1770s, it flourished as a tobacco port, declining in importance by the midnineteenth century. It continued as a cheap rent district until 1934, when Franklin D. Roosevelt's New Deal doubled government employment. Newcomers attracted by low prices and historical associations began purchasing property and refurbishing the area to recall its past. A committee was appointed to oversee all new construction and reconstruction to insure that Georgetown would retain its historical atmosphere. Restrictions paid off handsomely by inducing well-to-do families to inhabit homes along the area's quiet streets. When landlords tired of collecting exorbitant rents, they could sell their modest investments in history for sums often exceeding one hundred thousand dollars.

Nowadays, along with the maids and Mercedes flock pseudo-hippies, who crash in pads along the business streets at night.

During the day they roll out their sidewalk counters and peddle folk art of dubious quality, but they do provide an equalizing business force to the high-priced shops lining the streets.

Eighteen miles west of the capital in the rolling, well-forested hills of Virginia, Reston embodies a modern version of the concept of man in commune with nature. There, Robert Simon designed a self-contained suburb, where citizens of all ages could live, work and play without draining the resources of the nearby metropolitan area. A mixture of apartments, town and patio houses, and single family dwellings were grouped in clusters, surrounded by trees to create an illusion of uncrowded space— an idyllic suburb. But Simon soon ran out off cash and had to sell his dream to the Gulf Oil Corporation, which, to make a profit, set out to fulfill the projected population goal of seventy-five thousand as soon as possible. As fast as Gulf is building, the public is buying.

Designs lean towards sterile modern modules, which lend themselves to quick and economical construction techniques. Pseudohistorical bric-a-brac tacked on the exterior, and brick fences feed the need of nostalgic home buyers to feel that they are purchasing a substantial piece of old-fashioned housing. In response to criticism from friends, one resident defended his purchase by countering, "True, the construction isn't the best, but it's better than anything else we've seen in Washington's newly built suburbs and certainly less expensive." Despite government prodding to provide low-income and Federal Housing Authority financed housing, Reston is upper-middle class.

Those of meager finances remain trapped in the inner city, where progress in redevelopment has been slow. Old sections of Washington still have a few unpaved streets, littered with refuse from uncollected garbage, where the unemployed roam in search of drink or trouble. Although family income averages nine thousand dollars, welfare checks support many residents. Infant mortality is high. Those who make it past youth often succumb to pneumonia, tuberculosis or cirrhosis, common diseases of the poor, and, of course, the majority of statistics are written in black.

Between 1900 and 1910, Washington became the only city outside Africa with a predominently black population. Today blacks comprise 75 percent of the urban population and occupy 98 percent of the school desks. As in other cities, they have an unequal share of low incomes and poor education, even though this particular city is home to many of the oldest and wealthiest black families in America.

More than half of the nation's black physicians, lawyers, dentists, pharmacists, engineers and architects are alumni of Howard University, established in 1867 to provide education for newly emancipated slaves, but always an integrated institution.

Typical of the administrators at Howard is Joseph L. Henry, D.D.S., Ph.D., dean of the College of Dentistry. His lectures and messages to the student body are riddled with the militancy of emerging black power. He encourages his students to be not only professionally competent but "socially conscious, community oriented, politically informed and civically active." With a bit of professional humor he prepares students to "bridge the gap between the promises and reality and conditions existing in America today."

The College of Dentistry is anticipating difficulty. Foreign enrollment, which has always been high at Howard, continues, but black students are losing interest in the profession. Dentistry, medicine, teaching and the ministry were once the only avenues open to blacks reaching for middle-class status. Current civil rights activities have opened doors to other professions with less demanding requirements, and the federal bureaucracy has always provided better than average employment opportunities for blacks.

Not everyone in the capital works for the government. Those in service occupations far outnumber those in government, while others follow specialized occupations. They are the lobbyists and the government liaison experts. The former work for special interest groups, such as industries, agricultural organizations and conservationists, pushing and pulling congressmen to pass legislation beneficial to their clients. Government liaison experts, on the other hand, usually represent industrial firms, keeping their employers informed of up-to-the-minute opportunities for doing business with the government. They are frequently retired military personnel; industrialists apparently reason that no one is better qualified to deal with the government than Pentagon graduates, who for years managed to capture fifty cents of every tax dollar.

Their training ground on the Virginia banks of the Potomac is the world's largest office building. A rash of bomb threats has closed the Pentagon to the public, so that now only invited guests obtain permission to tread the rather spartan corridors.

There is not much to see. A few corridors are covered with a fine collection of World War II military art work, and tucked in one of the five corners of the five-story building, built in five concentric rings, is the Hall of Heroes. Spotlighted are enlargements of the nation's highest military decoration, the three medals of honor (army, navy and Marine Corps, air force), and flanking the display are the names of the men awarded the medal for serving their country above and beyond the call of duty. Generally the Congressional Medal of Honor, as it is called because it is conferred "in the name of The Congress of the United States," is bestowed on combatants, although several have been awarded to civilians in peacetime.

Portraits of past secretaries of defense hang in another corridor. Of the dozen men appointed since James V. Forrestal took the first oath of office on September 17, 1947, (sixteen months before his suicide), nine have held it for less than eighteen months. Almost all were military men, the only three with more stamina having been former presidents of major corporations. Proctor and Gamble's offering held out for a little over two years, while the former head of General Motors lasted four and one half years. Robert S. McNamara, once president of the Ford Motor Company, was the "winner," with an unprecedented seven years.

The Pentagon has long been the butt of jokes because it is a deep, deep well of Washington's vernacular, "bureaucratese." No other federal agency is as adept at stating so little by saying so much while using a maze of figures to establish points that would not pass muster with collectors of trivia.

Tangible evidence, if any is needed, is available on request (for ten cents) from the U.S. Government Printing Office in the form of pamphlet USASCAF PAM2, dated 4 October 1968 and entitled "The Pentagon." We found it the best adult comic ever offered for a dime; overblown patriotism riddles the opening statements, and with paragraph 4 numerical nonsense takes over: "The 30,000 employees arrive daily from Washington, D. C., and its suburbs over approximately 30 miles of access highways, pass 200 acres of lawn to park approximately 10,000 cars in 3 parking lots . . . 150 stairways . . . 19 escalators . . . offices that occupy 3,705,397 square feet . . . 4,200 clocks . . . 685 water fountains, . . ."

Americans, long accustomed to being numerically classified to death, will find little relief in reading the local tourist literature. Statistics filter into everything to impress visitors, native or foreign, with the scope of the capital, comparing everything in terms of how big, how much, how many. "The Capitol's floor area covers 162 acres and has 540 rooms. The Senate's Sam Rayburn Office Building cost $122,000,000 complete while the FBI's J. Edgar Hoover Building will cost about $126,000,000 for the shell alone. And the National Archives has enough records to fill 150,000 four-drawer filing cabinets."

Facts and figures seldom cease to flow even in points of minor interest. "Grant's statue in front of the Capitol is the world's second largest equestrian sculpture exceeded only by that of Victor Emmanuel in Rome." The only failure must be credited to the U.S. Naval Observatory, which, for all its scientific data, could only come up with a twenty-six-inch refractor telescope, "the largest in the D. C. area."

Escaping the bureaucratic tedium is easy for the visitor; he has only to pack his things and go. Until vacation time, Washingtonians rely on weekends for relief, but with an eye for the early start—Friday, at noon. Mellowed by martinis, office workers race off to some planned fate important enough to convince their department heads that quitting time should not be the standard 5 P.M. The plea guaranteed to obtain the fastest results starts with "I'm planning on driving to the coast."

Atlantic resorts are the favorite retreats of escapees fleeing the oppressive summer weather. Unfortunately, Chesapeake Bay lies between them and ocean breezes, and everyone knows that the shortest route lies across the Chesapeake Bay Bridge out of Annapolis. Therein lies the trouble—everyone knows! Traffic may back up for fifteen miles. To pass the time, people pack lunches and sports equipment and take advantage of the grassy banks along the highway.

First-class deserters fly away, either on domestic flights from Washington National Airport, near the heart of the city, or on foreign journeys from Dulles International Airport. The futuristic space missile launching site at the end of a twenty-seven-minute drive into Virginia is actually the Dulles terminal building. The airport's mobile lounges are a further example of impending destiny. After processing, 102 passengers are put into metal crates, which are then driven out to waiting aircraft. Untouched by human hands, prepacked for shipment: surely the concept is the one known to seamen as containerized cargo loading.

Those traveling elsewhere in the east coast megalopolis find the Metroliner from Union Station most efficient. America's fastest train makes it to New York City in three hours, give or take a few minutes. This is often faster than flying, because there is no baggage inspection, no circling for hours waiting for the opportunity to land, and the Metroliner deposits passengers in the center of town.

Their own backyard is where those who have been bitten by the excitement of controlling genuine horse power find deliverance. Horses are synonymous with Maryland and Virginia, and stables dot the landscape, generously supported by both novices and club members, who ride to hounds on Saturdays or play polo on Sundays.

Although conservationists severely criticize hunting as unfair to the fox, hunters feel that what was good enough for the father of their country is good enough for them. "George Washington hunted these hills regularly," mused a "hill topper" (a nonparticipant who watches the hunt from a vantage point). When asked how hunters fare today, the hill topper quickly stifled her laugh, then resumed in detached nonchalance, "Sometimes they catch one a season, but not usually that many." After the riders disappeared she broke her reserve and rather chummily confided, "Riders and hounds do look splendid physically, but mentally they are a bit lost."

While the horn of the huntsman sounded in the east, dogs

bayed to the west. A few riders ambled off northwards, and the hill topper spotted the fox sitting in a field to the south. "You see," she continued, "the hunt is really an opportunity to enjoy a ride through the country, jump a few fences and gossip with friends."

The hunt is a heritage from colonial days, when gentlemen farmers carried on the sport imported from Europe. The crisply cool days of autumn are the best. Sport shops accent the scenery with dollops of black and red riding habits. Sleek animals prance, and dogs, ears flapping, noses to the ground, run with agitated enthusiasm. Salutations are exchanged, reins tested, and the man with the tray dispensing champagne in long-stemmed glasses is called aside. The hunstman's horn pierces the air. Whether it is the social event of the season, the Potomac Hunt, when eighteenth-century carriages and costumes compete with the splendor of horse and rider, or the ordinary Saturday outing, it is the hunt. And it is thrilling!

An evening to equal the upper-class ambience of the morning hunt would have to be spent at the John F. Kennedy Center for the Performing Arts. Planned as a cultural meeting ground for the masses, its inconvenient location, expensive parking and high-priced theater seats have deeded it to the affluent.

Built entirely by subscription and donation, it is still far from finished. If it were not for generous gifts from foreign friends, the three theaters and grand foyer would be devoid of decoration. Nevertheless, a definite must is spending an evening beneath Austria's crystal snowflake chandelier in the Opera House. Japan's red and gold curtain need not rise, because the audience is often as good as the performance and definitely more outlandishly diverse in costume. Mink and levis, class and crassness are interwoven with threads of status consciousness, mod jargon of controlled euphemisms and occasional critical appraisals of what is happening on stage. A night at the Kennedy Center is a slice of Washington life as American as apple pie.

In the morning, Washingtonians work off the calories of the good life in the city's extensive parks, where America's official gardeners, the National Park Service, have laid out, and carefully maintain, paths and trails for joggers, hikers and cyclists. Cycling appears to be the most popular mode of eliminating the flab accumulated behind a desk.

"Bike Guide" is an informative pamphlet published by the National Park Service to aid pedaling enthusiasts in locating the forty-seven miles of bike paths. It also lists the dates of pending two-wheel festivals and races. The nation's first bike commuter trail was initiated in D. C., and today six thousand commuters use these facilities when weather permits, prompting big business to cash in on the boom. Parking lots rent spaces to cyclists, and a major car rental agency has begun dealing in wheeling.

The 708 parks and ninety-five memorials and statues in and around the capital are, of course, under the supervision of the National Park Service, and information on upcoming events appears in monthly bulletins but is also available from Dial-a-Park (426–6975). Most park programs are children oriented, such as the one at Pierce Mill, in Rock Creek Park, where eight to twelve year olds can learn in a two-hour workshop what it was like to grind cornmeal and whole wheat flour for a living.

Rock Creek Park, where Teddy Roosevelt used to ride horseback, covers $2\frac{3}{4}$ square miles along the course of Rock Creek. Running the entire length of the park, Beach Drive twists unmercifully as it follows the course of the creek, affording motorists, at least the ones not in a hurry, a picture window view of the four seasons. Nature lovers scorn the road and boast from their horses and bikes that motorists never really see the park.

Careful replanting has restored nearly all of the original forests, destroyed during the Civil War, but the fate of the early wildlife—bison, deer, bear, elk, wolf, and so on—has been less happy. In small numbers and well caged, they still exist in the National Zoological Park, which occupies 165 acres of the park. There, about twenty-five hundred birds and animals live out their lives in what might be called the national disgrace. As mentioned earlier, Congress disposes, and, as one sightseer snorted, "Apparently no congressman considered the zoo his pet project."

Yet, the design of the zoo's aviary is highly imaginative, and there are several distinguished guests, among them rare white Bengal tigers, Smokey the Bear, and two giant pandas, Ling-Ling and Hsing-Hsing. These two thoroughly pampered, furry creatures from the bamboo forests of western China are much more popular with the public then the latter is with them. Although they have an outdoor play area and are clownish by nature, they spend much of their time in small anterooms adjacent to their air-conditioned quarters. They also sleep a lot. Feeding time is when they can be seen best (if one can wedge through the constant stream of children).

The Chinese call them *hsiung mao* ("bear cat"), they are related to the raccoon family, and their appearance suggests that Ralph Nader induced mother nature to do a recall to correct the inefficiency of only two legs in the original design. However, the two paws, connected by a black stripe across the back, attached to the shoulders do little for their table manners. Bamboo, their natural food, and raw vegetables presented no problem, but rice, whose nutritional value to pandas is not apparent to the layman, ended up in their laps. And where, one wonders, would they get their rice cooked if they were still wandering the highlands of Szechwan and Kansu provinces?

Rock Creek's only other natural beauty competitor is Great Falls, eleven miles up the Potomac from the city. In addition to the thirty-five-foot-high waterfall and the Great Falls Tavern, there are locks from the abandoned Chesapeake and Ohio Canal. George Washington supported an earlier project (the Chesapeake and Ohio Water Project), believing that a water route between farmland around Cumberland, Maryland, and Georgetown, then a port, would be profitable. Construction was started in 1828; then for the first time in the nation's history, in 1834, federal troops were called out to settle a labor dispute. Crews of Irish, Welsh, English, German and Dutch worked on despite bad food, poor housing and disease, completing the 184-mile canal in 1850, but it was never a commercial success. The Baltimore and Ohio Railroad started construction the same day, finished first, and transported the bulk of cargo, which in the case of the canal turned out to be coal rather than produce. Following the closure of the canal to commercial traffic in 1923, the National Park Service took control of a few miles of the canal and made repairs, enabling sightseers to enjoy a leisurely journey on mule-drawn barges.

The end came in 1972. Whereas damage from previous flooding, a recurrent problem, had always been reparable, that left by Hurricane Agnes was beyond the financial means of the National Park Service to set right. But the canal had been so popular with local residents, as well as a steady stream of tourists, that the park service has been inundated by another kind of flood—offers of volunteer labor to reconstruct the canal. If the offers are accepted, the mules may someday be back in business. Gratefully, in Washington, where capital is usually used to mean money, some of her citizens still realize that the best things in life are free.

1-3. The banks of the Potomac River, first settled by Europeans in 1634, are now occupied mostly by parks and a maze of express highways. Washington, lying at the upper limit of navigation, is linked with the Virginia suburbs by several bridges: *previous page*, the graceful Arlington Memorial Bridge spans the river between the Lincoln Memorial and Arlington National Cemetery. *Left*, fishermen try their luck at sunset in West Potomac Park. *Below*, the river serves as a practice area for a racing crew from Georgetown University.

4-5. Newer government office buildings have been designe
to provide parking space, but it is inadequate. To reliev

sh hour traffic a limited express bus service using special
es of major highways has recently been established.

6-9. The several faces of law enforcement: the FBI prefers to avoid violence, but all agents prove their expertness at the bureau's firing range (*opposite*). Metropolitan policemen, like the city's bonded messengers, use motorcycles for maneuverability (*left*); horses are used for the same reason by U.S. Park policemen, who, along with National Park Service rangers, safeguard national monuments (*below*, *left* and *right*).

10-13. Georgetown has many fine restaurants and specialty shops; the shop at left caters to do-it-yourself gourmets. American diplomats are often graduates of Georgetown University, whose twin spires are prominent landmarks (*opposite*).

14. Major L'Enfant and George Washington are believed to have laid plans for the federal capital in Georgetown's Old Stone House, built around 1765.

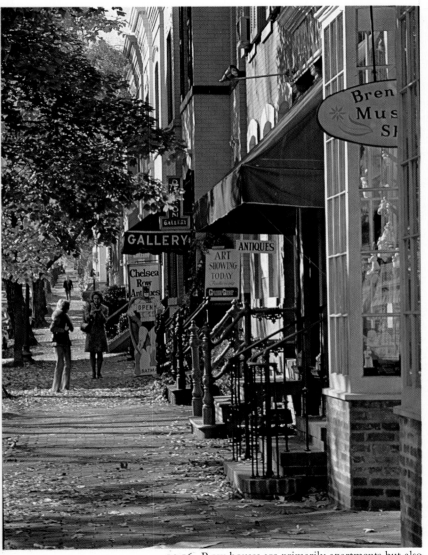

15-16. Row houses are primarily apartments but also house some of a seemingly endless variety of interesting shops found in Georgetown.

17. Scott Circle (*opposite above*) is one of the many circles and squares called for in the original design of the city; despite their aesthetic appeal, they tend to congest traffic.

18. Cruise ships docked in the Washington Channel (*opposite below*): the National Park Service vessel (*foreground*) plans its activities around youth groups from the Washington area.

19-20. At the Smithsonian Institution, an antique popcorn machine supplies edible evidence of successful technology. School buses occupy much of the parking space, although the Smithsonian sends exhibitions to local schools.

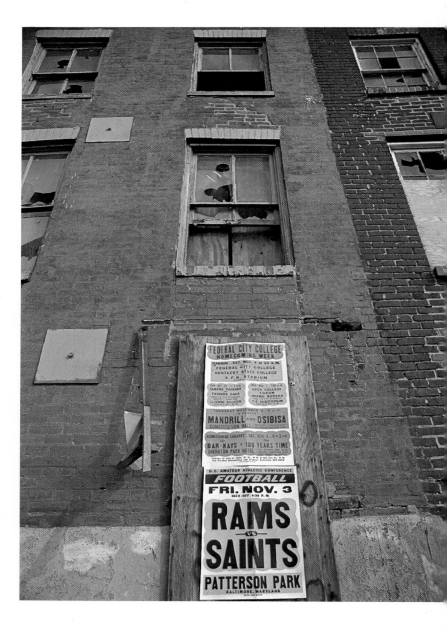

21-24. The view of 14th Street NW from the roof of Garfinkle's (*left*) and abandoned buildings destined for redevelopment are within a few blocks of the Capitol. *Overleaf*, L'Enfant Plaza was built as part of the comprehensive redevelopment plan for the area south of the Mall.

25. High-speed Metroliners reduce the time and increase the comfort of traveling between Washington
and New York City.

26. Nothing obstructs the view from Washington
Monument, by far the capital's tallest structure. This
is the south view, centered on the Jefferson Memorial.

29. The hunt, polo, and riding ▶ are popular on weekends in suburban Maryland and Virginia: *overleaf*, a hunt in Warrenton, Virginia.

27-28. Some areas of the Pentagon are dedicated to the preservation of military history. In the Hall of Heroes (*left*) are recorded the names of every recipient of the Medal of Honor. *Below*, a receptionist for the secretary of defense poses outside her office in the Eisenhower Corridor.

30-32. Washington's mild weather encourages year-round sports, but a visit to Alexandria's sailboat harbor suggests that parking is a problem not limited to drivers (*opposite*). *Left*, popular demand has induced the National Park Service to turn over segments of George Washington Parkway to cyclists on certain weekend hours. *Below*, on the Potomac bike path, it is time for a lunch break.

33-35. Denizens of the National Zoological Park, founded in 1889, have not been alone in feeling congressional penny-pinching, although the pandas have not done badly (*left*). They are much more dangerous than their cuddlesome appearance suggests. Birds inhabit an aviary remarkable for its good design (*below*).

36. Easy access to its recreational facilities is available to apartment dwellers along Rock Creek Park.

37-38. Pierce Mill in Rock Creek Park has been restored to operation by the National Park Service (*below*); *overleaf*, South Lane of Washington's Mount Vernon estate.

Three Branches

History is Washington's product, so to speak, yet very little of it appears to have been made by native sons. The only notable exception is in the world of music, where John Philip Sousa left his mark. Otherwise, the names in the history books belong to men and women born in the fifty states or, more rarely, the overseas territories: Puerto Rico, the Virgin Islands, American Samoa, Guam, the Trust Territory of the Pacific Islands, and the Panama Canal Zone.

The man who gave the Federal City its present shape was the one after whom it was eventually named. Some authorities regard it as George Washington's offspring.

Real estate, commerce and the military were but a few of the myriad of George Washington's interests. It was the death of his half brother Lawrence in 1752, when George was twenty, that launched him as a planter, first as renter and manager, but he was not to become sole owner of his half brother's extensive landholdings until 1761, with the death of Lawrence's widow, Anne Fairfax. Among the six inherited plantations, one was to become famous: Mount Vernon, known when George lived there as a youth as Hunting Creek, but renamed after Admiral Edward Vernon, under whom Lawrence had served in the Caribbean. Then, on January 6, 1759, Martha Dandridge Custis, a widow and one of the wealthiest Virginians of the period, and her two children, John Parke and Martha Park Custis, became his family (he had no children of his own).

The main house at Mount Vernon, built by Lawrence in 1743 on a rise two hundred feet above the Potomac, was the center from which Washington carried on his many activities. When he was there, he lived the life of the southern planter. Up at seven for breakfast, he spent the morning and early afternoon riding the countryside, hunting and checking on his farms, mills and other property. Dinner was at three. Bookkeeping or visitors, of whom there was a constant flow, occupied him until teatime, but he seldom joined guests for dinner, preferring to retire by nine.

Occasionally his ventures proved disasterous, but on the whole they were quite profitable. Foresighted and progressive, he invested in western lands and realized, as the majority of his contemporaries did not, the wisdom of soil conservation and the folly of reliance on tobacco as the sole crop. If other matters had not called him away, his astute management might have resulted in even more than the eight thousand acres and two-hundred-thousand-dollar book value of Mount Vernon at the time of his death in 1799.

Away from their estate, George and Martha's social life centered around a tavern known since 1796 as Gadsby's Tavern. Two dollars bought room and board consisting of two meals. Meeting rooms, sometimes the planning haunts of revolutionaries, were available for parties, while larger formal functions often found the Washingtons dancing in the second floor ballroom. When the Continental Army was placed in Washington's hands in 1775, he took over the tavern and turned it into his first military headquarters.

Following the last battle of the American Revolution (Yorktown, 1781), disgruntled Continental troops mutinied in Philadelphia in an attempt to recover back pay. Like all militant protestors, they shook up Congress, although not city and state officials, who refused to provide protection. The legislators decided to move to a place where they felt they could be in control, and move they did, assembling in eight cities in four states before reaching the new capital in 1800.

The problem of the debts of war dragged on for years. The treasurer, Alexander Hamilton, favored a plan whereby all costs were to be shared equally by the North and the South, but the latter was reluctant to cooperate, pointing out that most of the debts originated in the North. In the end, he and Thomas Jefferson worked out a compromise. The South agreed to pay provided that the North gave up its proposed sites for the Federal City. By 1791, George Washington had his way; the capital was to be carved out of a one-hundred-square-mile tract of Maryland and Virginia. He himself selected the sixty-nine square miles in Maryland, but he asked Congress to decide whether the other thirty-one square miles should be north or south of that site.

Of the nineteen landowners, all but one were reconciled to the fact that their fertile farmland was to become a city. David Burnes's land encompassed what today supports the White House, the Treasury Building, the Pan American Union, and parts of the Mall, the Ellipse and Pennsylvania Avenue. Sixty-six dollars per acre but no compensation for land designated for parks and roads was not a particularly good deal in his Scotch mind, nor could he foresee any profits to be derived from land he was allowed to retain, supposedly to be sold later as property values rose. He chased off Washington's emissary with words to the effect that the general would not have had much if he had not married the rich widow Custis. But eventually he relented.

Major Pierre Charles L'Enfant, French by birth, engineer and architect by profession, and a veteran of the American Revolution, was appointed to lay out the city. Brilliant as he was, he lacked tact in dealing with people of less imagination; within a year he was fired. Although he undertook other architectural commissions, execution of his sometimes grandiose plans continued to prove a problem, and he died in poverty in 1825. His plan for the capital, too, suffered a period of obscurity until the original manuscript was rediscovered in the office of geodetic survey in 1887. Subsequent city planning commissions, particularly one in 1902, have returned to it, and today the city reflects the spirit, if not the details, of his brilliance.

On an early autumn day in 1793, George Washington and a band of dignitaries formed the city's first official parade. Carefully the party stepped over rocks, maneuvered through thick elder bushes and gingerly forded streams via logs to reach the rise called Jenkins Hill. There, the Father of His Country became the "Father of the Capitol" by laying its cornerstone.

A prize of five hundred dollars, a gold medal and one city lot was offered for the design of the Capitol, but the competition ended without a plan that appealed to the selection committee. A few months later, Dr. William Thornton, a recent immigrant from the West Indies, belatedly submitted a plan that the critics acclaimed the finest. Although Dr. Thornton could not participate in the construction of the building—he was a doctor, not an architect—he stayed on to argue with the appointed architects, who wanted to incorporate their own ideas.

At almost the same time, work was begun on the Presidential Palace, as it was sometimes known unofficially, located in what had been David Burnes's orchard. A contest had been held, and this time the prize went to a highly regarded architect, James Hoban, who used the design of the seat of the dukes of Leinster, near Dublin in his native Ireland. And again, President Washington was more than instrumental. He established that such a building was necessary, selected the site and on October 13, 1793, laid the cornerstone. Construction was completed in 1799, the year of his death, and a portrait of him survives today as the only furnishing that has remained in the White House since its inception.

It was the custom in those days to complete the wings of a building before tackling the central portion. In 1800 the first section of the Capitol was enclosed in sandstone and ready to house the 32 members of the Senate, 106 from the House of Representatives, the Supreme Court, the Circuit Court, and the Library of Congress. Also from Philadelphia came the president, John Adams, various cabinet members and 130 government clerks to take up residence in the Federal City. Adams addressed the first joint session of Congress; his wife, Abigail, addressed letters to friends and relatives complaining of the appalling conditions of life in the city.

To accommodate the scattered population (variously estimated as being from three thousand to fourteen thousand) it was expected that residences would be built first, but instead a coach maker, a tinsmith, and other commercial enterprises took precedence. There were few places to stay. Even accommodations in Georgetown were inaccessible on rainy days when roads turned to mud and flooded creeks were impassable. Tiber Creek was the worst offender, but it had its saving grace. When floodwaters receded, potholes in nearby roads would provide catfish for the dinner table. In fact, wildlife in great abundance was the city's virtue. The makings of a feast were only a stone's throw from any point along Pennsylvania Avenue, and tasty they were, judging from the glowing reports of visitors.

Nevertheless, the inconveniences had Congress continually flirting with the idea of moving, while foreign delegations were equally spiteful of conditions. The British, and no doubt others, considered the new capital a hardship post and sent only bachelors as diplomatic representatives.

During August, 1814, both the Capitol and the President's House (it still had no official name) were put to the torch by British troops under the command of Rear Admiral Sir George Cockburn. While the British were being entertained by the destruction, divine providence intervened in the form of a hurricane-force wind. After flying bricks and collapsing roofs began killing the unsuspecting British troops, they beat a hasty retreat, to try their luck in Baltimore.

By September, everything had quieted down, except Congress. Once again it had lost control of a situation, and there were those among the legislators who thought it was time to move. Debate fermented; someone pointed out that it would look bad to the rest of the world if a foreign power had forced Congress to move. Whatever the reason, and the margin was thin, the move was voted down, a temporary brick capitol was built on the site of the present Supreme Court Building, and reconstruction began. The walls of both the Capitol and the President's Mansion were still standing, and liberal applications of white paint not only hid the scars but served to protect the rapidly deteriorating sandstone face of the Capitol. In 1818, the building that had already come to be popularly known as the White House was officially designated the Executive Mansion.

As the century's first quarter drew to a close, preparations were hastily being made for the return of an old friend, Marie Joseph Gilbert du Motier, the Marquis de Lafayette. Although many years had passed since he served under General Washington and he was then in his sixties, his welcome was that of a hero. A reception was held under the dome of the Capitol's rotunda. Heaped in glory, he received an honorary citizenship, an honor accorded to only one other foreigner, Sir Winston Churchill.

Lifting his glass, Lafayette toasted the city as "the central star of the constellation which enlightens the world."

To the more down-to-earth Virginians, the city was neither enlightening nor progressing rapidly enough commercially. In 1846 they requested and received back their portion of the one-hundred-square-mile district, which included Alexandria.

The first warnings of division were seeded, and reflected in a dispute over *Armed Freedom*'s headpiece. The design submitted to Congress by Thomas Crawford for the $19\frac{1}{2}$-foot statue for the dome of the Capitol included a cap similar to one worn by freed Roman slaves. That, objected Jefferson Davis, was an insult to the South, whose economy was based on slavery. The compromise this time was a helmet covered with a feathery eagle.

Construction work on the Capitol persisted, although not everyone was sure that the national motto, E Pluribus Unum ("Out of Many, One"), would. The Civil War was raging near the city, but when asked if work on the dome should be discontinued, President Abraham Lincoln thoughtfully replied in the negative. Across the Potomac, the Confederate flag fluttered over Alexandria, the boyhood home of Robert E. Lee, but the Capitol would be the symbol to the South of northern determination to remain as one (and its dome a model echoed in nearly all of the state capitols built after the war).

Surprisingly, the battlefield never came to the city; the sights and sounds of war did. Thirty thousand horses were corralled in the Foggy Bottom area. Thousands of troops trained in the city. Fondly nicknaming it the "Big Tent," three thousand of them bivouacked in the halls of Congress, from the basement of which wafted the sweet aroma of fresh bread. Two battles at Manassas (1861 and 1862) and one at Antietam (1862) turned the building into a fifteen-hundred-cot hospital. The influx of people brought pollution to Tiber Creek, which became a breeding ground for typhoid, scarlet fever and dysentery. By the time the dome was completed on December 2, 1863, it had been extravagantly christened in blood and tears.

April 14, 1865. Washington was still near hysteria with festivities. A few days previously, Pennsylvania Avenue had felt the feet of its grandest parade, as, for two days and nights, Union troops jubilantly marched to celebrate the war's end. At 10:15 P.M., in Ford's Theater, Abraham Lincoln's worries and weariness came to an end with a single, muffled shot and a demented cry of "sic semper tyrannis" ("Thus always to tyrants").

The capital, dusty under the hot sun and muddy when it rained, hung in limbo. Pigs were the chief sanitary engineers and Tiber Creek doled out its disease. Congress was, however, more interested in trying to impeach President Andrew Johnson than in building a city. Again it toyed with the idea of moving.

From 1871 to 1874, to counteract the influx of freed slaves, the city charter was revoked, to be replaced by a territorial form of government. After that, the decade brought improvements. The agent for change was the Governor's Board of Commissioners' Alexander R. Shepherd, a charming manipulator who soon became the "mayor" that the board elected so it would have a boss. Machiavellian in his tactics, and a bit of a scoundrel, Shepherd loved Washington but quickly tired of the constant begging that was the established way to get money from Congress. Through silver-tongued cajolling, he convinced the right people that it was time to pave the streets, put up street lights, turn Tiber Creek into Constitution Avenue and cultivate handsome parks. What he did not tell them was that his budget was only six million dollars. Sixteen million dollars over that figure was more than even the most clever bookkeeper could conceal from Congress, which disposed of Boss Shepherd. He headed for Mexico, but later was honored by the city for taking the initiative to do things that should have been done years earlier.

In 1871, the cornerstone was laid for the State–War–Navy Building. In keeping with Washington's pace, it took seventeen years to complete, but then it was the world's largest office building. With that title came the realization that the government was not about to construct such a pile of granite unless it meant to stay. From then on talk of moving almost ceased.

The new lease on permanency and better living conditions attracted the rich. Robber barons, eager to be close to the strings of government, which would help them bilk the public and rape the land's resources, began erecting their mansions in D. C., and the building boom was on.

"One supreme Court and . . . such inferior Courts as the Congress may from time to time ordain and establish" are the judiciary provided for under Article III of the Constitution. It would seem, however, that early congressmen and presidents regarded the Supreme Court as a third-rate power in the governing triangle. For a long time the presidentially nominated and Senate-confirmed justices spent their lifetime appointments tucked away in a rather unobtrusive corner of the Capitol.

Whatever the amenities, the role of the court in the governing process was soon subject to reinterpretation. Within two years of his appointment as chief justice in 1801, John Marshall issued the first (*Marbury* v. *Madison*) of a series of legal decisions that brought the Supreme Court to its rightful place as a coequal of Congress and the president.

Our own experiences with the arbiters of the law of the land were limited to photographing the marble exterior of the Supreme Court Building. But before the last leg of our tripod was extended, a guard walked over to check whether it bore rubber feet. "Mandatory requirement for all equipment set up on

Supreme Court property," he said suspiciously. While displaying our mandatory requirement, we asked if he had any interesting experiences to relate. "Nope!" he firmly but still suspiciously replied. "You have permission to photograph the building?"

While Milton went inside to obtain approval, I guarded our equipment and the guard kept an eye on me. Permission melted his gruffness, but after a few pictures we decided to move on to the legislative branch of the government. There, at least, if we got into trouble the resident authorities would not have the final say. Again our tripod was our means of introduction. "You'll need a permit to use it in the Capitol," we were told.

That one piece of photographic equipment has spawned a variety of regulations; boiled down, they come to three main points: in the Rotunda, it could be used only between 9 and 9:30 A.M.; a guard would have to accompany a photographer who had permission to use a tripod in the Senate or House wings; neither tripod nor camera could be used in either congressional chamber.

The first two rules, our guiding guard explained with one story. "According to rumors, a tourist tripped over a tripod set up in the Senate halls and sued the government for a bundle. The result was a ban on the casual use of them." An exception to the last regulation would, naturally, take an act of Congress; rarely has that happened. Official photographs of Congress are taken by staff members of the National Geographic Society.

"Restrictions began getting tough after 1954, when dissident Puerto Ricans started shooting in the Senate chambers," the guard continued. "Since then, the recent washroom bombing and numerous threatening phone calls have created tighter security measures and increased the police force. Too bad the Capitol isn't as easily accessible as it used to be. But the people have no one to blame but themselves."

Constantino Brumidi would have frowned on such violence.

A political refugee, born in Rome of Greek ancestry, he was so grateful to find freedom in the United States that he willingly decorated any surface the government deemed paintable in the Capitol. His profusion of fruits, flowers, animals, and birds drew us to the Senate wing first. His work, done primarily in fresco, although some oil paint was used, was coated with beeswax to protect it from the fingerprints of the curious.

Our guard had a sudden attack of softness as we entered the painted halls. "Look how well the colors have held up," he mused, as his eyes lovingly roved the walls and ceiling. "It's somewhat dark in here, but that helps preserve the color." Next he pointed out the patterned floor, "glazed Minton tiles from England." After relating a variety of historical facts, he credited a fellow guard with teaching him the fine details, and narrated his struggle through the ranks of the metropolitan police before gaining this much-sought-after appointment.

From the floor of the Rotunda, we slowly eyed our way 180 feet to the painting in the center of the dome. Brumidi began work in 1877 and was sixty years old when he lay on his back to execute the fresco of George Washington flanked by Liberty and Victory. Twelve years later, while working on the frieze along the base of the dome, he slipped and narrowly escaped death by clinging to the scaffolding. Within a few months he died.

His work was finished by Allyn Cox, who, at the age of seventy-six, is still at work. In February, 1973, Cox and two assistants began to change the "plain brown democratic walls" that the House had voted for its wing into scenes of nineteenth-century capital life, pictures of some of the state capitols and portraits of the Capitol's eight architects.

Our final stop, the meeting place of the House of Representatives until 1857, was Statuary Hall, so named for the stone and metal likenesses of prominent Americans. Each state is allowed to contribute two commemorative works of art. Georgia's Alexander Stephens, Utah's Brigham Young, Vermont's Ethan Allen, Idaho's George Shoup and South Carolina's John C. Calhoun are among the eighty-seven favorite sons and daughters now scattered throughout the House wing, since their combined weight would have been too much for Statuary Hall alone.

The distance to the soaring tip of *Armed Freedom*'s controversial eagle feathers is 287 feet, $5\frac{1}{2}$ inches, making the Capitol Washington's second highest point. Seventeen hundred and fifty gallons of paint long deceived everyone into thinking that the cast iron dome was marble. In fact the rest of building is sandstone; not until 1960 did Congress vote for a marble veneer.

"Completed" in 1830, the Capitol has actually never stopped growing, in keeping with the increase in the number of states, the number of congressmen, and the length of sessions, once scheduled from January to August but lengthened to a full year. Two new buildings for senators and their staffs and three for the House are all near the Capitol and interconnected by subway. Our short journey underground did not give us much time to think about the meeting with one of our state's senators.

Democratic and Republican public relations propagandists have always pushed the idea, "Come to Washington. See your senator." What they seldom bother to point out is that a congressman is usually extremely busy and cannot always see his constituents. Voters generally have to be content with catching a glimpse of him on the floor of the Senate or the House. But as Capitol guides will explain, congressional desks are frequently vacant for the actual work of Congress is done not in the meeting hall but behind the closed doors of committee rooms. What they, apparently, fail to point out is that most committee meetings are open to the public. But then legislators may be away, fact-finding or campaigning, or in their offices.

The last mentioned is where we sought to find out what kind of a man fills the senatorial mold. We knew the statutory requirements: he was one of two people elected per state to hold the office for a period of six years; he was at least thirty years old and a U.S. citizen for nine or more years. We also knew that his authority stemmed from Article I of the Constitution.

Experience has proved that elected officials tend to lack credibility. The harshest evaluators are inclined to divide the politician into three equal parts: spendthrift, promiser and potentate, all held together with a gift for verbalizing away lesser evils. Although the four traits are shared by any number of politicians, some do have a sincere interest in good government.

With those thoughts in mind, we sat in the office of Adlai Stevenson III, wondering which virtues or vices our State of Illinois representative might possess. Our first impression was that he certainly did not spend many of the taxpayers' dollars on decorating his reception room, a tiny space crowded with two enormous desks, a few pieces of furniture, piles of papers, books, pamphlets and the ubiquitous potted plants characteristic of all federal agencies. Then, a somewhat nervous aide bounded from behind thick wooden doors, which we assumed concealed the senator's elaborately decorated, lavishly furnished inner sanctum. There was a short explanation of how busy the senator was, a plea to take as little time as possible, and, to our surprise, we found ourselves in a group of offices as crowded as the reception area. For a few minutes the aide disappeared; on returning, he reiterated his plea to keep the visit short.

Shock awaited us. The senator had neither the inclination nor the finances to support an Arabian nights' atmosphere. Covering the walls were Illinois memorabilia—certificates of merit and etchings depicting the good old days—prominent portraits of Abraham Lincoln and the senator's father, Adlai Stevenson II.

whose grandfather, Adlai Stevenson, was vice president from 1893–97, under Grover Cleveland. An attractive fireplace and a few pieces of well-worn furniture completed the decor.

Behind the desk in the midst of this middle-class splendor sat one of the one hundred chosen gods of Jenkins Hill in unadorned raiment—shirtsleeves. He was attacking a stack of the ever-present papers, books and pamphlets. "I know you'd like to take my photograph," he said quietly, while clutching a fistfull of papers, "but I'd find it inconvenient to clean off my desk at this moment." Milton assured him that we wanted him to be au natural.

"Eighty percent of a senator's job consists of answering inquiries from constituents," he said, as he signed another paper after careful scrunity. For fifteen minutes we all worked, only our camera shutters and his scratching pen punctuating the stillness.

When we finished, he gratefully offered a cliché about the session having been painless. For a politician, we found his restrained manner disconcerting, but during the ensuing small talk he discovered that we liked to travel, and, suddenly, the man became more like we had expected. True to the image, he began to do all the talking. He spoke of his feelings about some of the things his fact-finding travels had revealed, frustrations over various government policies, both national and international, and a not too subtle party plug. He wound up by giving us a few insights into his job: "often too much for one man to handle . . . because of this burden I can't always achieve the satisfaction of completing a job the way I feel it should be done . . . peripheral duties consuming time better spent on problem solving."

Teasingly I inquired, "Does that mean you won't run for another term?"

Jolted a bit, he quickly recovered and mischievously responded, "No, no! Don't get me wrong! I love this job."

Illinois has the reputation of electing some pretty dubious characters to run its local affairs, but Senator Stevenson is typical of those we have put in federal offices. Not only does he care about his job and the people he represents, but, most important, he strives to make the government better. The three equal parts of this particularp olitician are wrapped up in the gift of gab. But three virtues instead of four possible faults are election results that should make any voter happy.

We did not ask him whether Article II of the Constitution ("The executive Power shall be vested in a President . . .") was of any interest. In this day and age, the presidency may no longer be the dream of every American boy, but surely a senator must harbor some thought of it.

The objective, 1600 Pennsylvania Avenue, is only 1.2 miles away. All the presidents except Washington have lived there. After being vacated for three years after the British roasting, the need for structural repairs accumulated until 1948. It would seem that, beyond the physical state of the building, President Harry S. Truman grew weary of rumors of Lincoln's ghost wandering the halls, mysterious knocks on doors and footsteps without visible means of support. Truman and family occupied Blair House, across the street, workmen exorcised the spirits by ripping out the bowels of the structure, and, since then, there have been no accounts of things that go bump in the night.

Of the 132 rooms in the White House, as President Theodore Roosevelt had Congress legislatively title it, 54 of them and 16 baths on the second and third floors are exclusively for the First Family. The rest are offices, dining, ball and sitting rooms for a variety of official functions. Lincoln's bedroom takes the prize for notoriety. Reserved for visitors, it has an anecdotal history involving some of the world's most distinguished recumbents.

Senator Stevenson's father slept there, but unable to bring himself to lie on the eight-foot-long bed of the great president, he spent an uncomfortable night on a handy couch. Unknown to him, the couch had been a favorite resting spot of Lincoln, while doubts persist as to the authenticity of the bed.

Tourists see but a few "color-coded" choices of gold, green, blue and red. We were drawn to the gaiety of the Red Room, long the favorite of first ladies. Although each has left her personal mark upon the house, none has affected it as much as Dolly Madison and Jacqueline Kennedy.

Mrs. Madison exercised her benign influence for sixteen years, first for widower Thomas Jefferson and then for her husband. A young widow at the time she married the future president, she was a credit to plain gals in that her beauty radiated from within. Her vivacious personality made her the undisputed hostess with the "mostest," a title modern claimants have yet to usurp. With the British hot on her trail she commanded courage enough to calmly pack and save what White House property she could.

Mrs. Kennedy possessed the kind of beauty Dolly Madison lacked, and no war sent her packing. She strived to restore to the White House many of its rightful furnishings and, through her elegant and restrained tastes and insistence on historical accuracy, made a showplace of America's number one home.

Red and white predominated during our tour. Christmas was near, and the halls were decked, almost stuffed, with poinsettias. "This is the best time to see the White House," said an aide. "In another week there will be the evening candlelight tours, when the rooms are only lit by tapers and blazing fireplaces. It's very romantic."

There was a time when "going to Washington to see the president" was no empty remark. In the beginning, the White House was open twenty-four hours a day, and anyone so inclined met with little opposition, such as the drunk discovered one morning snoozing on a couch. And Andrew Jackson's exuberant followers were so excited about his winning the presidency that they stormed the mansion and literally drove its new occupant away. But now the security barrier around the White House has turned the remark into a hollow joke.

"Where you headed today?" a friend unthinkingly inquired one morning, as she scanned her newspaper.

"To the White House to see the president," we replied.

Returning her attention to the paper, she unconsciously remarked, "Well, say hello for me."

Her lack of interest put a damper on our enthusiasm. Milton had patiently waded through the letters and telephone calls connected with getting anything done in D. C. In this case, they terminated with the secretary to the secretary of the White House press secretary. In exchange for a time and date for our appointment, we dutifully submitted our names, address, dates of birth, heights, weights, color of eyes, color of hair and social security numbers for a security check. Still, it was a relatively simple procedure on our part, and one not requiring the imagination displayed by an authoress of John Q. Adams's day who wanted to interview the president. Knowing that he liked to swim in the Potomac, she waited discreetly until he entered the water. Then she sat on his clothes until he finally consented to an interview ninety minutes later.

I would never go all the way with Milton. Stopped by a sudden attack of the flu just as we reached the Mall, I fed the voracious parking meter, while Milton and twenty-five pounds of camera equipment finished the assault on the White House. Apparently, too, I had fallen under the capital's very own miasma. I began to recall facts and figures on the thirty-seven men who have taken the oath of office forty-six times.

What kind of a man is elected president? Critics rank Abraham

Lincoln as the best (and least attractive) and Warren G. Harding as the worst. William McKinley was the stuffiest, Franklin D. Roosevelt, the most self-assured, and for laughs, no one beat clowning Calvin Coolidge. Theodore Roosevelt was the youngest at forty-two, although John F. Kennedy was only one year older and five others were under fifty. Twenty-four were lawyers, ten were former generals, and four, Lincoln, James A. Garfield, McKinley and Kennedy, were assassinated.

Being "born poor" was regarded as a source of virtue, and four candidates possessed the ultimate claim of having been born in log cabins. Yet none of them was among the poorest by the time he reached the top. Money, whether for electioneering or feeding a family, has been a source of trouble for many candidates. Ulysses S. Grant, McKinley and Truman were the poorest, and in Truman's case it was his presidential salary that finally made him financially secure.

The job has never been easy, and presidents in moments of despair have offered their personal perspectives: John Q. Adams, "The four most miserable years of my life . . ."; Lincoln, "I feel like the man who was tarred and feathered and ridden out of town on a rail. . . . If it wasn't for the honor of the thing, I'd rather walk."; William Taft, "This is the loneliest place in the world." In contrast, Teddy Roosevelt's family enlivened the premises as has no other chief executive's. Sincerely he boasted, "No other president ever enjoyed the presidency as I did."

Milton, meanwhile, found himself surrounded by members of the press waiting to photograph the president and a group of Russians in town to sign a trade agreement. For over an hour he had the chance to study the faces of men who form the communications link between the president and the electorate. He was prepared to be disappointed. "The president frequently changes his mind," a press aide had forewarned.

An amplified voice sang out, "Gentlemen, it has been decided that no photographs will be allowed this morning." Low rumbles emanated from the group. A few left.

Fascinated by the news media's telephones, typewriters and teletypes, Milton wandered around a bit longer before deciding to leave. He had one arm in the sleeve of his coat when the voice made another announcement. "There is a change in this morning's schedule. A press pool will be allowed to photograph. AP will represent the wire services, the *Washington Post* will cover newspapers, Kyodo News Agency for the foreign press, NBC ... the BBC ... and Milton Mann."

The nonchalant newsmen were taken aback by the last name but quickly recovered to voice their objections to being left out. The chosen few jockeyed for position, while Milton nervously stood off to the side, next to a Secret Service agent. Not knowing the lighting situation, he asked, "Is flash permissible?"

"Sure!" replied the agent.

Noticing that similar equipment was missing from pressmen's cameras, he asked a press aide the same question and received the same answer.

When the doors swung open, the press invaded the inner sanctum like a tidal wave, then stopped short around a group of men in business suits sitting in arm chairs. By the time Milton gingerly entered, he found little space for him and his cameras.

While all around shutters clicked furiously, he began hunting for an angle to show the president surrounded by members of the press. Unfortunately the press was more interested in taking pictures than being in them. Before he could release his shutter, a man stepped in front of his camera. The same thing happened again. The Secret Service agent at the door solemnly announced, "You have sixty more seconds, gentlemen." Milton fumbled with a lens, noted that no one was using a flash and snapped off a couple of frames. "Thirty seconds left, gentlemen." The guard sounded like impending doom. Suddenly a draft rushed into the room, TV lights went out, and there was another pronouncement. "That's all for today, gentlemen."

Milton stumbled out in a daze; cornering a newsman he inquired, "Why didn't anyone use a flash?"

"Well, we think the president doesn't really like it," came the answer.

Back at our friend's home that evening, the entire family was pouring over local newsprint. Absentmindedly, one inquired about our day.

"Said hello to Dick," Milton replied, "but Pat was too busy to see us."

A page turned and one of the assembly looked up patronizingly. "Why, Milton, you have on a suit."

Milton, not one to wear such attire except for a very special reason, brought all reading to an abrupt halt. "We really did see the president," he proclaimed weakly.

When the flurry of excited questions subsided one youngster wanted to know, "How much time did you spend with the president?"

Milton reflected, tallied up the pronouncements of the Secret Service agent and came up with a grand total of "a minute and a half." It did not seem like much, considering the phone calls, security checks, equipment examinations, waiting, rejection, the announcement and ultimate achievement, but his ninety seconds with Nixon is still the most popular story he tells of our visit to Washington.

39-43. The Capitol as seen from the Mall (*preceding page*); *opposite*, the hallways painted by Constantino Brumidi are a highlight of the Senate's wing; *overleaf*, tour groups gather under the dome of the Rotunda (*left*); the House of Representatives used to meet in Statuary Hall (*below*).

44-45. The view north from Washington Monument: the White House, like the Capitol, is a complex of buildings built at various times. George Washington, during whose first term the cornerstone of the main building was laid, is the only president not to have lived there. Although the exterior has changed little, successive presidents, and first ladies, have left their mark on the interior, to the point that it became structurally unfit for occupancy in 1948 and had to be rebuilt. Walls covered in magenta silk make the Red Room the brightest spot in the White House (*overleaf*).

The People's Choice

Foreign travel posters touting Asia's and Europe's ancient history have always played successfully on the American inferiority complex, traceable, supposedly, to being a nouveau culture. And there are those who acknowledge international second-class citizenship, tending to forget that there may be an advantage in the shortness—only two centuries—of the republic's history.

Annually, some eighteen million tourists forego the rest of the globe's historical offerings and flock instead to Washington, the Mecca of democracy. The number is not particularly significant (Atlantic City attracts about sixteen million annually), but perhaps the reason is. Justices of the Supreme Court are far from being the only ones who professionally second guess the revolutionary founders of the republic. Presidents and legislators, historians and journalists, among others, do it. And even the citizen at large feels a chummy rapport with men like Washington, Franklin, Jefferson, great grandfathers on our ancestoral tree, far less remote than many another national hero. Moreover, while the decisions of history have been barbaric as well as heroic, ignorant as well as intelligent, disastrous as well as brilliant, as have those of older and supposedly wiser civilizations, the visitor no doubt senses in the national capital a revitalizer of the ideals upon which the nation was founded.

Busloads of school children on spring vacation are the advance guard, popping up, with the crocuses, by the buildings and around pigeon roosts that become visual aids to their history courses. Tirelessly they tramp the Smithsonian, are overwhelmed at the sight of millions of new dollars rolling off the presses, and stand in awe as an agent of the Federal Bureau of Investigation explains how the organization nearly always gets its man.

Spring also brings a burst of cherry blossoms and older students who have read their history and have an intense desire to rewrite some of the basic assumptions. Disillusioned with a government they feel apathetic to fulfilling its ideals, they rally on the Washington Monument grounds, picket the White House or mass silently at the foot of the Lincoln Memorial. Their frustrations were summed up best by an Indian spokesman directing a recent foray on the Bureau of Indian Affairs. With great satisfaction he noted, "For once, we're in the fort while the government is running around us in circles."

Summer brings an onslaught of families. Shunning expensive accommodations like Watergate, they head for the neon corridor of low rents and McDonald burgers, U.S. Route 1. Their cars aggravate an already deplorable traffic situation. Visitors returning to Wyoming will extol the virtues of the city, but not without recalling the vices of rush hour traffic, lack of parking space, abundance of ticket-writing officers and a system of road signs as complicated to decipher as hieroglyphics. Traffic signs denoting changes in direction and parking restrictions at variable hours put a premium not only on the ability to tell time but on the faculty for making rapid calculations. Then there are Major L'Enfant's squares and circles. Aesthetically pleasing, they are, but drivers dismiss them as damn nuisances. Washingtonians suffer all these things, and more. Fender bumpings are so frequent that the majority of insurance companies refuse to cover many residents. Many a marriage, it is said, has hit the courts when the pilot handed a Washington road map to his navigator wife. The completion of the Metro, which should alleviate some of the problems, is some years in the future. Until then, visitors may find taxis and tourmobiles the sensible way to sightsee.

Our touring of D. C. started at the peak. Washington Monument is so prominent that, as several male residents told us, wives rely on the 555-foot needle as if it were the North Star. When lost, they drive to its base for reorientation.

Echoing the capital's on-again off-again way of doing business, it little resembles Robert Mills's original design, a birthday confection with one gigantic candle in the center. The two shades of its stone face are the result of a political quarrel in 1854, which stopped construction at the 150-foot level for a quarter of a century. President Grant finally put the project back in motion by approving federal funds for its completion. Then, although the same pits were the source of the marble, it came from different strata and, of course, weathering has not been uniform. The result, nevertheless, is a majestic tower of strength, starkly devoid of decoration and relying solely on nature for adornment.

To get to the top, we took the elevator (one minute and ten cents). Because park rangers cannot spare the time to rescue the climbers who never make it, the National Park Service no longer allows climbing of the 898 steps to the summit.

Originally nothing separated the viewer from the view, but after the fifth suicide windows were installed. By prearrangement, they were opened for us by a ranger, and looking down to the neatly clipped lawn, we found it difficult to imagine the thousands of cattle penned there during the Civil War. Imagining people was unnecessary; they were there, a constant colorful stream. How many of them, we wondered, would join the endless ranks of souvenir-hunting vandals who have caused inestimable damage to public buildings by irrationally thinking that as taxpayers they have the right to deface government property. Currently the choicest morsel is Kennedy Center.

A pleasant respite from the rings of people around Washington Monument was the Jefferson Memorial, across the Tidal Basin, where few visitors seem to go except in answer to a call of nature, the Cherry Blossom Festival, which occurs sometime in April. The trees, two thousand of them originally, were a gift from the city of Tokyo in 1912. After World War II, cuttings were sent to Japan, and today the trees struggle for existence in the smog of both cities.

Rudolph Evans's bronze statue of Jefferson, Declaration of Independence in hand, appears to enjoy the quietude; confident in manner, Jefferson seems to command the viewer to read his words carved on the surrounding walls. He was, among other things, a great lover of books, and is reputed to have read all of the books published in the English language during his lifetime. A good conversationalist but a poor public speaker, he preferred to accomplish his objectives through writing and diplomacy. He believed in freedom of mind and body and the need for education, and he appreciated the need for laws and democratic institutions to change with changing times.

Tens of thousands of men who died in America's battles lie in the Fields of the Dead, the major part of Arlington National Cemetery. The property was once part of Arlington Plantation, owned by George Washington Parke Custis, grandson of Martha Washington (and adopted son of George). It was inherited on Custis's death in 1857 by his daughter, Mary Ann, who had become Mrs. Robert E. Lee in 1831. While Lee spent much of his time on military assignments, Mary Ann and their seven children resided at Arlington House, high on a hill overlooking Washington. The family left Custis-Lee Mansion a month after

Lee's departure on April 20, 1861, when he, along with three hundred of the army's seven hundred officers decided that their hearts lay with the southern cause. After the government confiscated the land for failure to pay back taxes, two hundred acres were set aside as a burial ground for the Civil War dead, but it was 1883 before the government made compensation.

Like all cemeteries, Arlington is for the living, who come to pay homage to the well known or to read with curiosity the words carved on the grave markers of the lesser known. There are also frequent military funerals, lending their special dignity to death as the color guard marches through fields of white headstones and, equally poignant, the hourly changing of the guard at the Tomb of the Unknowns. The task of honoring the unknown soldiers from two world wars and the Korean War fittingly falls to volunteers from the country's oldest infantry unit, the Third Infantry Regiment, known as the The Old Guard.

In the military line, Washingtonians consistently recommend the Tuesday night summer program at the U.S. Marine Corps War Memorial, the reproduction in bronze of Joseph Rosenthal's Pulitzer Prize winning photograph of the raising of the Stars and Stripes on Mt. Suribachi, Iwo Jima, on February 23, 1945. The sculpture, commemorating one of the Marine Corps' bloodiest battles (5,550 dead, 17,000 wounded), honors all marines who have given their lives since the establishment of the corps in 1775. In gold at the base are the words of Fleet Admiral Chester W. Nimitz, "Uncommon Valor was a Common Virtue."

The view from Washington Monument looking over the Lincoln Memorial, across Arlington Memorial Bridge, past the eternal flame at President Kennedy's grave and up the summit to the Custis-Lee Mansion is, undoubtedly, one of the inspiring vistas envisioned in Major L'Enfant's original plan. His own remains are part of that unbroken line of memorials, resting, since 1909, beneath a table-shaped gravestone on the front lawn of the mansion. Incised on the marker is his design for the city.

In examining city statuary commemorating men, we found none that compared with the single figure dedicated to a woman. We had read and heard much about *Grief*, but were hardly prepared for its overwhelmingly ethereal quality. It is regarded by many critics not only as Augustus Saint-Gaudens's masterpiece but as one of the finest sculptures in America, and Harry Truman, perhaps alone among presidents in taking an active interest in his temporary hometown, considered it and Lincoln's statue in the Lincoln Memorial the only two sculptures in the city worth seeing.

The death of his vivacious wife, Marian, in 1885 stunned historian Henry Adams (grandson of John Q. Adams). Their marriage, of twelve years's duration, was considered ideal, and at the time relatives only noted in their letters that "she died under peculiarly tragic circumstances." Biographers believe she committed suicide after a period of depression. *Grief*, standing in contemplative seclusion among holly bushes in Rock Creek Cemetery, is her memorial, but *Grief* is only the popular name. We found the name that Saint-Gaudens gave it, *The Peace of God*, more appropriate, for the sculpture transcends things earthly, capturing effectively what the artist wanted to convey, a feeling "beyond pain and beyond joy."

Art is to be found in galleries and museums throughout the city, but the finest collection of the last eight centuries of European art, indeed one of the outstanding collections in the world, is that of the National Gallery of Art, one of the twelve bureaus of the Smithsonian Institution located in the capital. The gallery, which dates from 1941, owes its existence to one of the robber barons, Andrew Mellon, who bequeathed to the people of the United States his collection of "only finest quality" art and funds for a building to house it. His request that the building not be named for him has been honored, but the collection is known as the Mellon Collection. Others have followed his example, as he hoped they would, by donating their valuable collections, which may be freely copied and photographed. Artists may even request the use of easels and stools.

All the libraries, repositories and galleries in the country would be hard pressed to match the mind-blowing experience of spending a few hours in the museum's museum, the Smithsonian Institution, or more exactly, the Museum of History and Technology and the Museum of Natural History, which together make up the U.S. National Museum. The Smithsonian inherited its name under the terms of the will that made it possible, that of the English chemist James Smithson. Because Smithson's nephew died heirless, the fortune was to be used "to found at Washington . . . an Establishment for the increase & diffusion of knowledge among men."

Why the United States, which Smithson had never visited, was to be his benefactor is a question that has never been answered, but a reluctant benefactor it was. For nearly a decade, Congress argued, often bitterly, about the gift. According to Senator John C. Calhoun of South Carolina, acceptance would be "unconstitutional and in any case beneath the dignity of the U.S." Finally it relented and established the institution by one of its acts on August 10, 1846 (Smithson died in 1829, his nephew, six years later). The money had arrived in Philadelphia in 1838, in nine boxes, each containing 1000 gold sovereigns in 105 bags, and one box with 960 sovereigns, eight shillings and a sixpence. The Treasury paid interest at the rate of 6 percent per year.

The brownstone main building completed in 1855 housed all the exhibits for the first twenty-five years. Fieldwork financed by the Smithsonian brought in the first exhibits; subsequently

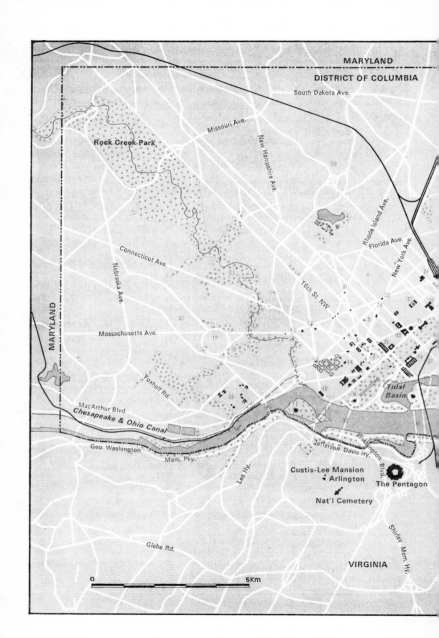

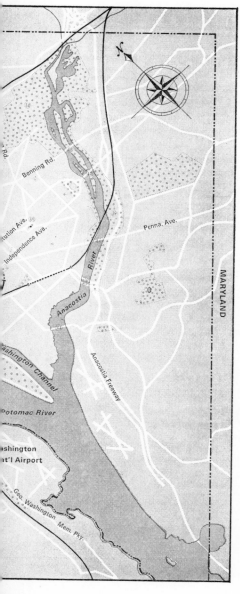

District of Columbia

1. Washington Monument
   The Mall
2. The Ellipse
   Zero Milestone
   The White House
   Executive Office Bldg.
   Treasury Dept.
   Blair House
3. Lafayette Sq.
   St. John's Church
   Botanic Gardens
4. Farragut Sq.
5. Franklin Sq.
6. Scott Circle
7. Jefferson Memorial
   East Potomac Park
8. Lincoln Memorial
   West Potomac Park
9. Pan American Union
   Red Cross
   Corcoran Gallery of Art
   Dept. of Interior
   Bureau of Indian Affairs
   Civil Service Commission
   Federal Reserve Board
   Nat'l Academy of Sciences
   State Dept.
10. Kennedy Center
11. Theodore Roosevelt
    Memorial Park
12. Georgetown Univ.
13. Washington Circle
    Geo. Washington Univ.
14. American Univ.
    U.S. Information Agency
15. Dupont Circle
    Dupont Theater

(*continued overleaf*)

Washington Gallery of
Modern Art
16. Sheridan Circle
17. Islamic Center
18. Dumbarton Oaks Park
19. U.S. Naval Observatory
20. Cathedral of St. Peter & St.
Paul
Washington Cathedral
St. Sophia Cathedral
21. Nat'l Zoological Park
22. Dept. of Commerce
23. Dept. of Justice
Nat'l Archives
Federal Bureau of
Investigation
Ford Theater
Smithsonian Portrait Gallery
24. Greyhound Bus Terminal
25. Mt. Vernon Sq.
26. Nat'l Gallery of Art
27. Judiciary Sq.
28. Dept. of Labor
29. Union Station
Columbus Fountain
U.S. Gov't Printing Office
30. The Capitol
Senate Office Bldg.
Supreme Court
Library of Congress
House of Rep. Office Bldg.
31. Logan Circle
32. Howard Univ.
33. Catholic Univ.
34. Nat'l Arboretum
35. Lincoln Park
Emancipation Monument

36. Bureau of Engraving &
Printing
Dept. of Agriculture
37. L' Enfant Plaza
Freer Gallery of Art
Smithsonian Institution
38. Nat'l Aeronautics & Space
Administration
Dept. of Health, Education
& Welfare
Voice of America
39. Anacostia Park

Bridges

40. Francis Scott Key
41. Theodore Roosevelt
42. Arlington Memorial
43. Geo. Mason Memorial
Rochambeau Memorial
44. Frederick Douglas
45. Anacostia
46. John Philip Sousa
47. E. Capitol St.
48. Benning

they came from many sources. War Department survey teams looking for railroad routes into the interior enlarged the collection, as did various national institutes, the Patent Office, private exploration, individual contributions and gifts from foreign nations. Presently, exhibitions cover over one million square feet, while others of the fifty-nine million cataloged items are in warehouses scattered throughout the country. Besides Smithson's remains (moved there in 1904), the original castlelike building contains offices and a Visitor's Information Center, where one can learn what each building houses.

To those whose interest is religion, the city offers twelve hundred churches, of all faiths and in a profusion of styles ranging from the frugal Federal style of St. John's to the gothic grandure of Washington National Cathedral. The former, on Lafayette Square opposite the White House, has for more than a century and a half been the president's church, and a pew, number fifty-four, is reserved for the first family. Stained glass predominates in this small, impressively restrained church, designed in 1816 by Benjamin Latrobe, one of the Capitol's architects. It well fulfills the claim that Latrobe wrote to his son: "I have completed a church that has made many Washingtonians religious who had not been religious before."

Washington National Cathedral is impressive for the engineer and architect as well as the admirer of beautiful buildings. Large columns extending deep into the earth and a steelless framework support the entire structure of Indiana limestone, and, according to recent National Bureau of Standards' structural tests, should continue to do so without major structural repair for the next twenty centuries. A purple-robed guide reminded us that we were still in Washington by quoting the estimated cost of construction (forty million dollars), but what is more impressive is that it is probably one of the last structures of religion to be embellished by artists who have lovingly donated their time for the glory of God. The builders have not rushed; the foundation stone was laid in 1907 and completion is expected in 1985.

A variety of artistic mediums has been used. As a needlepoint enthusiast, I found the kneeling cushions in the War Memorial Chapel of particular interest. Church members have volunteered their time to creat mini-yarn masterpieces in red, white and blue, depicting important events, places and men in American history.

Also outstanding in the potpourri created by devout craftsmen is St. Sophia's Greek Orthodox Cathedral, where artists are mosaicking the entire interior of the building. Glittering gold accentuates the old world style of the designs and Greek letters. When completed, St. Sophia's will be a ceramic pearl.

In the Islamic Center, whose minaret overlooks Rock Creek Park, the mosque stands at an angle to the outer building, which, in typical American fashion, is parallel to Massachusetts Avenue. The reason for this is to be found in the Koran, which requires that both the mihrab (usually a niche, but sometimes a plaque) and worshippers when they pray face Mecca. Nowadays, the muezzin no longer announces from the minaret the five times daily when Moslems are required to offer prayers. He was the victim of an unneighborly solution to what nearby dwellers termed "noise pollution."

The neighborhood is very international, for this is Embassy Row. Lining Massachusetts Avenue are embassies and chanceries of about one quarter of the city's more than one hundred diplomatic missions, which lend an international air in celebrating their national holidays, in wearing traditional garb and in adding their tongues to the variety heard in the streets from other visitors.

The only one open for public tours is the Iranian chancery, but then most of the diplomatic corps would agree with the Indonesian staff member who answered our request to photograph what goes on behind the closed doors by explaining that "there is really nothing to see. It's all work." In the case of his embassy, he was only partially right. Like the majority of legations, the Embassy of Indonesia happens to be housed in a former mansion. This particular one is noted for its beautifully carved grand straircase, but otherwise only the ballroom, equipped for traditional Indonesian music and entertainment, is noteworthy.

The differences between a consulate, an embassy and a chancery were explained to us by a Japanese embassy official. "We have ten consulates across the U.S.," he said. "They help Japanese visitors or immigrants to America with problems that arise, and they also issue visas and information to Americans [and others] planning to visit Japan. The chancery contains government offices, while embassy generally means that there is an ambassador in residence." Embassy also refers specifically to the ambassador's residence, and a legation is a mission of less than embassy rank. A consulate general is a large or important consulate, and while activities such as economic and political reporting are carried out at all levels, government to government contacts are strictly at the embassy level.

In the garden of the Embassy of Japan, in a natural setting of trees, plants and rocks bordering Rock Creek Park, nestles the 100-Year Anniversary Tea House, designed and constructed in Japan by master craftsmen. On special occasions when the tea ceremony is performed in this atmosphere of calmness, the scene is enlivened by the delicate patterns of the kimono of wives of embassy staff members. "They do protest a bit though," confided the Japanese official. "There isn't a dry cleaner in the U.S. who will purge the dirt from their kimono afterwards according to Japanese standards." The garments have to be returned to Japan, where they are completely disassembled before cleaning.

The fluttering of flags over Embassy Row made us think of

our own flag, unfurled daily over buildings around the world in the State Department's far-flung network. The nation's first and perhaps most popular diplomat was Benjamin Franklin, whose intelligence and astuteness impressed his European male counterparts, while his charm captivated the females. The desk on which he, John Adams and John Jay signed the Treaty of Peace in Paris in 1783 now stands in the John Q. Adams State Drawing Room on the eighth floor of the State Department Building.

It is unfortunate that the area is not open to the public, for it contains outstanding examples of eighteenth-century furnishings and crafts. Besides the drawing room, there is an enormous dining room and several more intimate meeting and dining rooms, all tastefully decorated. It is also the only place in our experience where the ladies' and gentlemen's lounges are decorated with paintings, Oriental carpets and silver. However, the accumulation of objets d'art is not due to any special wealth of the department; rather it is the work of the Special Fine Arts Committee, which arranges for the donation or loan of art treasures from private collections.

For the public, there are tours of the building's lobbies, one of which contains the flag of every nation with which we have diplomatic relations. In another one is an exhibit of gifts that foreign admirers have presented to members of the Foreign Service. To prevent recipients from being unduly influenced the department prohibits their retention, catalogues and stores them. But they are returned to the diplomat when he retires.

At the same time that Congress changed the Department of Foreign Affairs into the Department of State in 1789, it made the secretary of state the custodian of the Great Seal of the United States, which until that time had been under the care of the secretary of the Senate. Demonstrations of the seal, part of the regular tour for school children, are given by the administrator of the seal, presently Mrs. Bernice Renn. It is, as she explains, "the symbol of the nation's sovereignty [and] is applied to official documents by the secretary of state after he has countersigned the papers with the president." It also appears on military ornaments, such as buttons, cap insignia and medals; government publications; flags; and odds and ends, such as State Department stationery and matchbooks.

Unofficially, the obverse design of an eagle clutching an olive branch in one claw and thirteen arrows in the other was quickly incorporated into patterns for everything from furniture to tableware, although today commercial use is rather limited. Both the obverse and the reverse designs remain unchanged from those approved by Congress in 1782, but the reverse design is seldom used; perhaps the only use of both designs is on the back of the dollar bill. In fact, because of the impracticability of impressing both sides on paper, the die for the reverse design has never been cut. By itself merely an attractive pattern, the seal becomes impressive when imprinted on a round waferlike piece of paper that is glued to an official document. Among examples in the lobby display are presidential proclamations, treaty ratifications and commissions granting individuals power to represent the government.

Documents, some bearing the seal but most without, destined for permanent preservation are kept in the National Archives Building, construction of which was finally authorized by Congress in 1926. There in the center of the main hall are the big three: the Constitution, the Bill of Rights and the Declaration of Independence. They fare better now in the building's controlled environment—no windows, special lighting, air conditioning and controlled humidity—than they ever have previously. All three are badly faded, the Declaration of Independence almost to the point of illegibility. In line with modern techniques of preservation, the cases are filled with an inert gas, helium in this case, and in the event of a disaster, a hydraulic system would deposit the entire exhibit in the earth below the building.

The Library of Congress uses similar methods in preserving two of its most valued treasures, the Gutenberg Bible and the Giant Bible of Mainz. The invention of movable type goes back to China some four centuries before Gutenburg's time, and, in Europe, it was invented in Holland, but Johann Gutenburg is generally credited with having improved the process, particularly typecasting. Around 1450 he printed two hundred copies of the Bible, of which forty-seven are still extant. The one in the possession of the Library of Congress, considered to be in perfect condition, is one of only three complete copies. We, however, preferred to gaze at the beautiful Giant Bible of Mainz, handwritten on the finest, whitest, oversized sheets of velum.

The library was established on the principle that if congressmen were to govern effectively, they would need access to important books and periodicals, but in the years since its founding in 1800 it has expanded enormously to serve the nation and is one of the world's great libraries. Since it was located in the Capitol, it was destroyed in the War of 1812, but once again funds were allocated, and Thomas Jefferson's personal collection of books was purchased to form the nucleus of the new library.

We found the main building's ornate architecture a welcome relief from the usual run of government buildings. It dates from 1897 and is the work of the army's Corps of Engineers, which, one suspects, had help in creating the interior's delicate Italian Renaissance touches. From the visitors' gallery overlooking the octagonal main reading room, we scanned the art work silently. From the main level rose the subdued rustling of turning pages, as readers made use of one or another of the thirty thousand volumes at their immediate disposal, which must be used on the premises. The library's collection, totaling some eighty-five million pieces, consists of books and magazines, records, maps, photographs, drawings, tapes, and pieces of music. Anyone desiring to read what Thomas Jefferson read, or any of thirty thousand other valuable books, can do so in the Rare Book Division.

Lectures and concerts, listed in the Calendar of Events, are also part of the library's offerings. Most popular—seats are priced at twenty-five cents—and tremendously well received are the recitals given weekly from October through April in the Coolidge Auditorium. From cases in front of the theater, guest artists often select one of the Stradivariuses on display.

We cornered a guide to inquire whether the report that the library houses a copy of every book ever published was true. Specifically, we were interested in bolstering our egos with the knowledge that our own first publishing accomplishment was there. Politely but pointedly he answered, "probably not." Contrary to popular belief, neither all the world's books nor all those published in the United States are collected. "The library," he continued, "chooses volumes it feels will be of interest to the general readership or books with literary merit and educational value for scholars. What we do have, however, is a nearly complete card catalog, which other libraries and educational facilities use as an encyclopedia of published books."

We followed him to a section of the main catalog. There in one of the seemingly endless drawers of cards we found our book listed, but when the guide skeptically offered to see if the volume actually sat on the shelves, we declined. We were satisfied with that plateau of accomplishment and did not want to deflate our pride by knowing the library's evaluation of its content.

Having gained an idea of what the government collects, we headed for the building where money is mass-produced. The story of the country's money, however, does not begin with the Bureau of Engraving and Printing, which dates from 1862, when six people in the attic of the Treasury Building performed the task of overprinting seals and signatures on one and two dollar bills privately printed under government contract. By 1877, all paper currency was rolling off presses in Washington.

The first printing of currency was authorized in July, 1775, and was followed within a few months by the establishment of the Treasury Committee to oversee the accounting of public funds. As the republic grew and prospered, the Department of the Treasury did what all bureaucracies have a habit of doing: it spawned bureaus, most of which dealt with bookkeeping and gained little publicity. Others, such as the Bureau of Customs, the Bureau of the Mint, the Savings Bond Division, the Internal Revenue Service, the Secret Service and the Bureau of Engraving and Printing became familiar to the public.

An official was assigned to guide us through the security checkpoints and locked doors to the area where high-speed intaglio printing presses were running. Our attention was immediately drawn to the neatly stacked sheets of dollars, thirty-two bills to the sheet, that the machines were spitting out. "This year we produced 3,107,000,000 pieces of money with a face value totaling $21,095,000,000," the official said.

Suddenly one press stopped. A bit of inquiry revealed that the chrome-plated plate from which bills are printed had cracked. "We can run about four hundred and fifty thousand copies before something happens to the plate," the official continued. "They are made from steel engravings, an expensive process but difficult for counterfeiters to duplicate."

Dollies stacked with bills were wheeled around us. We sought a less busy area where we could continue our lesson. "Notes take a total of fifteen days to produce at a cost of eight-tenths of a cent per. One-dollar bills make up two-thirds of the production and have the shortest circulation life-span, of about eighteen months. Five-dollar bills last twenty. We have only two customers for our product: the U.S. Treasury, which uses the money to pay government debts, and the Federal Reserve Bank. The Federal Reserve Act of 1913 established the latter in order to give the U.S. a more elastic currency. It also serves to help control inflation, deflation, and improve supervision of banking throughout the country. Of the $62,598,770,882 currently in circulation, 98 percent of it is in Federal Reserve notes."

Noise indicated that the press was again in operation. "Sure glad to see that," he said. "We're in the middle of our Christmas rush and working around the clock to print enough money to satisfy holiday shoppers."

Currency comprises only 25 percent of the nation's money supply; checking accounts hold the bulk. Even government debts once settled with notes of five-hundred-dollar, one-thousand-dollar, five-thousand-dollar and ten-thousand-dollar (no longer printed) value are now paid by check.

Surprisingly, the bureau ran in the red for a number of years. "Presses cost half a million dollars each," continued our informant, "and it wasn't easy to convince those who balanced the budget that new equipment meant better and more economical production. Money isn't our sole output. We also produce bonds; public debt securities; food, revenue and postage stamps. ... it was postage stamps and a group of philatelists that bolstered our petty cash fund into the black."

Stamps, first issued by the U.S. government in 1847 and, like currency, privately printed, have been the bureau's business since 1894. Presently, 26.7 billion are printed annually, with rolled stamps, because of their convenience, accounting for one-third of the production. The bureau also produces precanceled stamps for business firms planning large mailings.

Commemoratives, of course, are what cause the gleam in the philatelist's eye, and the first U.S. issue, in 1893, commemorated the discovery of America. Recognizing the fact that stamp collecting is big business, the government sets up display booths at philatelic conventions, with, occasionally, curious results.

Some years ago, in the name of public relations, several thousand cards featuring an outdated stamp and information about its history were printed. Although they were free, there were few takers. After lying unwanted in odd corners of the bureau's offices and being dragged out for several subsequent conventions, they were finally snapped up at a foreign show after being canceled with the date and the place where they were distributed. It was the cancellation, of course, that did the trick. Soon, because the government could not afford to keep up with the demand, it began charging for the cards. And that is one way that collectors help support the equipment that makes their hobby possible. "Would you believe," said the official, shaking his head, "that the original souvenir no one wanted recently sold at an auction for two hundred and fifty dollars?"

The Bureau of Engraving and Printing employs three thousand people, and every office manager spoke proudly of his workers, referring to them naturally as craftsmen and artists. The question of honesty in the face of blatant temptation was shrugged off by one manager, who replied, "After a year, employees think of money only as work." We pressed the interrogation, curious to know what happens before that year has passed. Reluctantly he admitted that a few had tried to take home samples but quickly added that the Secret Service tracked them down.

At the time of the establishment of the Secret Service in 1865, "funny money" constituted a third of all money in circulation. Detection of counterfeiting and forging of government bonds, checks and so on, is still its main concern, but in 1901 its mandate was widened to include protection of the president and his family, the vice president and, more recently, some political figures. Occasionally, agents are assigned to guard works of art or historical documents in transit. Still, though he is efficient and highly regarded, the T-man does not capture the imagination as does public lawman number one, the agent of the Federal Bureau of Investigation.

The group of special investigators that the Justice Department established in 1908 was reorganized in 1935 as the Federal Bureau of Investigation, for the purpose of investigating violations of federal law, collecting evidence in cases in which the United States is or may be the interested party, and performing duties specifically directed by Congress or the president. Bank robbers, kidnappers, extortionists, spies and bombers are among those who draw the attention of the bureau, not to mention illegal users of the Smokey the Bear emblem.

Agents are somewhat special among law enforcement officers in that they must possess a degree in either the law or accounting. They are also graduates of a fourteen-week course at the FBI Academy in Quantico, Virginia. Working hours are long, travel and relocation, frequent, but 49 percent of the agents stay with the bureau for ten years or more.

Trepidation overcame us as we entered the bureau. Like the Canadian Mounties, FBI agents have a reputation for getting their man. Phone calls made to arrange our visit did little to ease our minds since they always started with, "Yes, Mr. Mann, we know *all* about you."

The giant agent at the door scrutinized us, then, with charming command, requested permission to inspect the contents of our belongings, right down to the inside of our cameras. Then an even taller agent appeared and with a furtive glance announced that he would be our guide. We decided the moment was ripe to confess the stealing of a paper napkin bearing the name of the place where we had dined the previous evening. "That's not in my jurisdiction," he said, smiling ever so slightly. At least it appeared to be a smile.

Our tour began with the sensational aspects of the organization's early history, when bullets and criminals were as pesky as flies. Our hometown, Chicago, is held in special affection. At the fingerprint display we learned that there were 197,713,711 on file, but not because there are that many criminals. Besides the military, there are many federal jobs where fingerprinting is a requirement, as well as, in some cases, state and local government positions and occupations such as the merchant marine. There are also people, such as frequent travelers and people who suffer from amnesia, who volunteer to be fingerprinted.

The Ten Most Wanted list caught my eye because of the females it contained. One was allegedly a bomber. "Political sympathy is often with such people, making our job more difficult," noted the agent. "People on the list may not be the worst offenders against society. Professional criminals often stay out of public view. Selections for the Ten Most Wanted are made on the basis of past records, seriousness of their present crime, how much of a threat they pose to the immediate community and whether or not nationwide publicity would assist in their apprehension." Since its initiation in 1950, the list has been instrumental in bringing about 294 arrests, 101 of them through information given by private citizens.

"One man was apprehended with the assistance of a honeymooning couple," the agent explained. "They had stopped in Washington for a while. As part of their sightseeing they took the FBI tour. Later, while strolling around Niagara Falls, they recognized a face from the Ten Most Wanted they had seen on the tour and informed the local FBI office."

Besides handling its federal responsibilities, the bureau assists municipal police authorities through the computerized National Crime Information Center. Telecommunications equipment instantly speeds data on wanted persons and descriptions of stolen property to law enforcement agencies throughout the United States and Canada.

The agent is the romantically visible face of the bureau; the scientific and technical specialists of the FBI laboratory are its unseen detectives. It is sometimes the technicians—spectrographers, mineralogists, handwriting experts, ballisticians, and so on—who bring to justice the culprit who thought he left no clue. Fingerprints on a tomato, a postage stamp irregularly torn and paper matches have been some of the offbeat items that have taxed their scientific ingenuity to provide documented evidence leading to a conviction. Authoritative files cover such things as typewriter standards, automobile paints and watermarks.

Twenty-three agents have lost their lives to date. The official weapon is a .38-caliber revolver, but agents must also prove their proficiency with a 12-gauge shotgun, a .347 magnum revolver, a .45-caliber submachine gun and a .308 rifle. On the firing range, another agent gave proof of his proficiency. One could say that our tour ended in a blaze of glory as the machine gun discharged its nineteen rounds in two seconds. And another two duly impressed citizens walked away convinced that crime does not pay, particularly at the federal level.

Nothing in Washington compares with the magic of the Lincoln Memorial, nor are there under the heavens many structures that impart the spiritual qualities found in this monument in classic Greek temple style. Inside, Daniel Chester French makes us see the Civil War president not only as a man of authority but also one of love and grief. Lincoln appears uncomfortable, almost questioning why a temple of elegance exists for one of simple ways. He seems embarrassed at the sea of visitors ebbing around his feet and pleads with them to stop looking and instead read what he had to say. Carved on the south and north walls are his Second Inaugural Speech and the Gettysburg Address.

We chose to stand in the presence of the latter. Half hidden in a row of columns, we watched with fascination the effect the sculpture had on those who stood before it. They slowed, then stopped and stared, brought to hushed whispers by the overwhelming power of the work. Overhead a flock of birds fluttered from the main hall into the somewhat isolated area where we were. Knots of people dispersed, emulating the birds, until they too stood before Lincoln's words. Uncomfortably they began to shift the weight of their bodies as the meaning struck their minds. How many times before had they read the Gettysburg Address? Or memorized it as children? Inaudible murmurs filled the air as they mouthed the words, as if praying. For the first time it had become meaningful.

For a moment we saw many Americans, members of a society of shut doors and guarded hearts, brought to the point of tears. In this imposing hall, the softly repeated words echoed magnificently in their simple eloquence, glorifying the nation's soaring ideals and the heights it had attained, muting the praise with the reality of its weaknesses, but ever hopeful for the future.

A father with three children entered and broke the spell. For some reason he felt compelled to read aloud to his children what he felt they should know: "Fourscore and seven years ago our fathers brought forth on this continent a new nation, . . ."

"But, Daddy," piped up the littlest, "I can't remember all those words."

"You will," he confidently responded.

IN THIS TEMPLE
AS IN THE HEARTS OF THE PEOPLE
FOR WHOM HE SAVED THE UNION
THE MEMORY OF ABRAHAM LINCOLN
IS ENSHRINED FOREVER

46-47. The awe-inspiring likeness of Lincoln was thought by
President Truman to be one of the capital's finest sculptures;
overleaf, morning fog over the Potomac.

◄48. Washington Monument is as strong as it looks, swaying only one-eighth of an inch in a thirty-mile-per-hour wind.

49. Excerpts from his writings, carved in white Vermont marble, surround the heroic statue of Thomas Jefferson.

51. *The Peace of God,* or *Grief,* is the work of the Dublin-born Augustus Saint-Gaudens (1848–1907), who revitalized American sculpture. Rock Creek Cemetery, where it is located, is part of the 260-year-old parish of St. Paul's.

50. and 52. Arlington National Cemetery was established in 1864 on land confiscated from the Custis-Lee family because of the Civil War; restitution was finally made, in 1883, on the basis of a Supreme Court ruling. The grave of Major Pierre Charles L'Enfant (*below*) dates from 1909; he died in poverty in 1825.

53-55. Well-known churches: opposite is Washington National Cathedral, whose style is fourteenth-century Gothic, and below is the National Shrine of the Immaculate Conception; the stained-glass windows at left are in St. John's, the "president's church."

56-57. The minaret of the Islamic Center towers over Rock Creek Park. Friday, the day for praying at the mosque, brings Moslems from many nations.

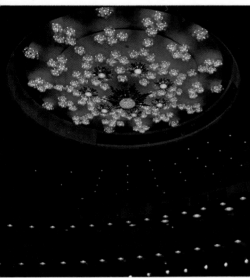

58-61. The John F. Kennedy Center for the Performing Arts, opened in 1971, may have required many more years for completion had it not been for the generous gifts of many nations; the snowflake chandelier in the opera house was donated by Austria (*left*). The exterior balcony, with its fountains and trees, is popular with strollers (*opposite above*); *opposite below*, the concert hall and, *below*, the grand foyer in the late afternoon sun.

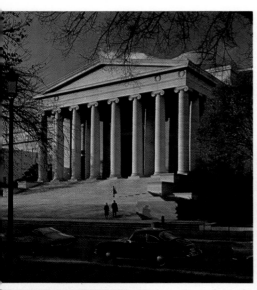

62. Performances are still held in Ford's Theater, where President Lincoln was assassinated (*opposite*).

63-65. The National Gallery of Art collection of European masters is outstanding. The world's largest marble structure, it has several interior gardens.

66-67. Expensive to maintain, many mansions have escaped the wrecker's ball by being turned into embassies; *opposite* and *left*, the Embassy of Indonesia.

68. The 100-Year Aniversary Tea House in the garden of the Embassy of Japan was prefabricated and shipped from Japan.

BLE

69-72. The Library of Congress, main reading room (*opposite* and *below*): the dome fresco by Edwin Blashfield is *The Evolution of Civilization and Human Understanding*. The Gutenberg Bible, given to the library in 1930, is a perfect three-volume edition.

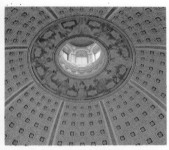

73. These microbiologists are among the top-ranking American and foreign scientists at the National Institutes of Health.

74. The independent Federal Reserve Board is responsible, among other things, for regulating the domestic money supply.

75. This secretary works for the American Red Cross; many national and international organizations are headquartered in and around the capital.

76. All new dollar bills are meticulously checked; then the sheets are cut and stacked into bricks of four thousand bills.

77. At the National Oceanic and Atmospheric Administration, a hydrometeorologist scans charts in pursuit of Washington's favorite weather—rain.

78. All tracking and measurement data from space flights are telemetered through Goddard Space Flight Center, which also originates space research: *opposite*, the master control room during a space flight.

79. The Voice of America broadcasts shortwave radio programs twenty-four hours a day from its master control room. The broadcasts are in thirty-seven languages.

80. Senator Adlai Stevenson III answers his share of the two million letters per month received by members of Congress.

81. Mayor Washington confers with members of his staff. The city is governed by Congress, rather than its citizens.

82. The secretary of state receives foreign dignitaries
in the department's John Q. Adams room.

THIS BEAUTIFUL WORLD